Computer-Aided Problems to Accompany

Basic Marketing

Fifth Canadian Edition

by

E. Jerome McCarthy, Stanley J. Shapiro, and William D. Perreault, Jr.

1989

IRWIN

Homewood, Illinois 60430
Boston, MA 02116

CONTENTS

ACKNOWLEDGMENTS

Steven A. Griffin played a significant role in this project. Drawing on his extensive experience in developing computer-aided "courseware," he contributed many creative suggestions that helped to shape the design of the PLUS program that accompanies this problem set. More significant, he did all of the PASCAL programming for PLUS. He shared our ambitions for what PLUS could be--and worked closely with us through many revisions to ensure that the program was both flexible and easy to use. We value his talent and his many contributions to the project.

Linda G. Davis also made important contributions. She contributed ideas for several of the problems. She made many good suggestions for ways to improve early drafts of the instructions for the PLUS program--and helped in revising the messages on the help screens that appear in the PLUS program. She also helped prepare the camera-ready copy for this booklet.

We would also like to thank all of the marketing faculty and students who worked with earlier versions of these problems and the PLUS program. Their suggestions helped us to improve the final product.

Computer-Aided Problems to Accompany Basic Marketing

GUIDE TO THE USE OF THESE PROBLEMS

The problems in this book--and the accompanying computer program that you will use to solve them--were specially developed to accompany the Fifth Canadian edition of McCarthy, Shapiro, and Perreault's *Basic Marketing*. The computer program is named *PLUS*--an abbreviation for *Professional Learning Units Systems*. PLUS is similar to other programs that marketing managers use to analyze decisions--but it is easier to use. A "master" diskette with the computer program and all of the problems is available to instructors from the publisher.

A suggested computer-aided problem is listed at the end of each chapter (except the last one) in *Basic Marketing*. Each of the problems focuses on one or more of the marketing decision areas discussed in that chapter. The earlier problems require less marketing knowledge and are simpler in terms of the analysis involved. The later problems build on the principles already covered in the text. The problems can be used in many ways. And the same problem can be analyzed several times for different purposes.

While it is not necessary to do all of the problems or to do them in a particular order, you will probably want to start with the first problem. This "practice" problem is simpler than the others. In fact, you could do the calculations quite easily without a computer. But, this problem will help you see how the program works--and how it can help you solve the more complicated problems that come later.

COMPUTER-AIDED PROBLEM SOLVING

Marketing managers are problem solvers who must make many decisions. Solving problems and making good decisions usually involves analysis of marketing information. This information is often in numbers. For example, a marketing manager needs to know how many customers are in the target market--and how many units of a product will be sold at a certain price--to estimate how much profit is likely to be earned with a marketing strategy. Marketing managers also analyze marketing-related costs--to help control their marketing plans.

Many marketing managers now use personal computers to help them analyze information. The speed of computer calculations means that a manager can look at a problem from many different angles. He can see how a change in one aspect of his plan may affect the rest of the plan.

The computer can only take a manager so far. It can help keep track of "the numbers" and speed through tedious calculations. But, the manager is the one who puts it all together. It takes skill to decide what the information means.

The computer-aided problems that accompany *Basic Marketing* will help you develop this skill. Most of the problems are short descriptions of decisions faced by marketing managers. Each description includes information to help make the decision. The information for each problem is in the PLUS computer program. There are several questions for you to answer for each problem. You should use the computer program to do an analysis. But most problems ask you to indicate what decision you would make--and why. Thus, in these problems--as in the marketing manager's job--the computer program is just a tool to help you make better decisions.

SPREADSHEET ANALYSIS OF MARKETING PROBLEMS

Marketing managers often use *spreadsheet analysis* to evaluate their alternatives--and the PLUS program does computerized spreadsheet analysis. In spreadsheet analysis, costs, revenue and other data related to a marketing problem are organized into a data table--a spreadsheet. Spreadsheet analysis allows you to change the value of one or more of the variables in the data table--to see how each change affects the value of other variables. This is possible because the relationships among the variables is programmed in the computer. Let's look at an overly simple example.

You are a marketing manager interested in the total revenue that will result from a particular marketing strategy. You are considering selling your product at at $10.00 per unit. You expect to sell 100 units. In our PLUS analysis, this problem might be shown in a (very simple) spreadsheet that looks like this:

Variable	Value
Selling Price	$10.00
Units Sold	100
Total Revenue	$1000.00

There is only one basic relationship in this spreadsheet: total revenue is equal to the selling price multiplied by the number of units sold. If that relationship has been programmed in the computer (as it is in these problems), you can change the selling price, or the number of units you expect to sell, and the program will compute the new value for total revenue.

2   McCarthy, Shapiro & Perreault

But now you can ask questions like: "What if I raise the price to $10.40 and still sell 100 units? What will happen to total revenue?" To get the answer, all you have to do is enter the new price in the spreadsheet and the program will compute the total revenue for you.

You may also want to do many "What If" analyses--for example, to see how total revenue changes over a range of prices. Computerized spreadsheet analysis allows you to do this quickly and easily. For example, if you want to see what happens to total revenue as you vary the price between some minimum value (say, $8.00) and a maximum value (say, $12.00), the program will provide a What If analysis showing total revenue for 11 different prices in the range from $8.00 to $12.00.

In a problem like this--with easy numbers and a simple relationship between the variables--the spreadsheet does not do that much work for you. You could do it in your head. But, with more complicated problems the spreadsheet program can be a big help--making it very convenient to more carefully analyze different alternatives or situations.

USING THE PLUS PROGRAM

Don't worry. *You don't have to know about computers to use the PLUS program!* It was designed to be easy to learn and use. The program will give you "help" information whenever you need it.

A Menu Box Gives Directions--and Help

When you use the program, information is displayed on the computer's screen. The screen looks different in different parts of the program. But every screen has a "menu box" at the bottom. You will want to pay attention to the menu box because that's where the program displays directions for you.

The directions in the menu box are brief. The first few times you use the program you may want more help than these summaries provide. This is not a problem. In the menu box you will see the word Help--and the letter H will be "highlighted." If you press the H key (short for the Help command) on the computer keyboard, a screen with more detailed instructions will quickly appear. This quick help information is specific to where you are in the program.

If you still have a question after reading the Quick Help Screen, look in the menu box and you will see the phrase "General Help." Again, the letter H will be highlighted. If you press the H key again, a General Help Menu

Screen will appear. It offers more information. Select the topic you want and the information will appear on the screen. When you are finished with general help you can press the R key (to "Return to the Program" where you left off). Remember, you can get back to this "general help" from any point in the program. Just press H to get the Quick Help Screen, and then press H again to get the General Help Menu Screen.

Along with the Help command, the menu box also has other words or phrases that summarize different commands--what you can do at that point in the program. Here, as with Help, just press the key for the highlighted letter to select the command you want. For example, on some screens you will see the phrase Quit--and the letter Q is highlighted. If you are finished with your work, press the Q key and the program will end. Don't worry about accidentally hitting the Q key and losing your work. Before the program actually ends, it will ask you if that's really what you want to do and you will have to press another key to end the program.

IMPORTANT! Try things out. A mistake won't hurt anything! If you press a key that isn't useful at that point in the program, the computer will beep at you or display a message. In that case, just check the message in the menu box--or the help information--and try again! The following pages give some additional instructions--but all of the information you need is available by simply pressing the H key. So, you may want to go ahead and try the practice problem now--especially if you've used a computer before.

Start at the Problem Selection Screen

When you use the program, the first screen displayed is the Title Screen. By pressing any key you will move on to the Problem Selection Screen--the real starting point of the program. The Problem Selection Screen shows a list of problems. The problem at the top of the list will be highlighted. In the menu box at the bottom of the screen, you will see the phrase "Work Highlighted Problem" and the letter P will be highlighted. If you want to work the problem which is highlighted on the list, simply press the P key, and the program will display a short description of the problem you selected. A longer description of each problem appears in this book--and is necessary to actually do the problem.

If you want to work another problem on the list--instead of the highlighted one--look again at the menu box at the bottom of the Problem Selection Screen. You will see the phrase "Highlight Down" with the letter D highlighted and "Highlight Up" with the letter U highlighted. Press the letter D to move the highlighting down to the next problem on the list. Press the D key again to move even further down the list. Pressing the U key will move the highlighting up the list of problems.

IBM personal computers have special keys labelled with left, right, up and down-pointing arrows. You can also use these special arrow keys to move up or down the problem list. If you've never used a computer, you will probably find it useful to look at Appendix A at the end of these instructions. It provides a labelled drawing of a typical keyboard for an IBM personal computer--and briefly explains the purpose of the special keys. It shows the normal location of the arrow keys and other keys mentioned in these instructions.

On the Problem Selection Screen, you will also see a small down-pointing arrow near the bottom of the list of problems. You will see an arrow like this on other screen displays as well. The arrow means that additional information is available--but won't all fit on the screen at the same time. For example, on the Problem Selection Screen the down-pointing arrow means that the list of problems continues beyond what you see on the screen. To bring the additional information onto the screen--continue to press the D key (to move "highlighting Down"). Similarly, you will sometimes see a small up-pointing arrow on the screen. When this appears, you can use the U key ("Highlight Up") to move back to the top of the information. The special keys marked PgDn (which stands for "Page Down") and PgUp (which stands for "Page Up") can also be used when the down arrow or up arrow appears on a screen. The best way to see what they do is to try them out when a small arrow appears on the screen.

From the Problem Selection Screen to the Problem Description and Spreadsheet Screens

Once you select a problem from the Problem Selection Screen, a Problem Description Screen will appear. This gives a brief description of that problem. Then you can continue to the Spreadsheet Screen for that problem by following the menu box instructions. The spreadsheet displays the starting values for the problem.

Each spreadsheet consists of one or two columns of numbers. Each column and row is labelled. Look at the row and column labels carefully to see what variable is represented by the value (number) in the spreadsheet. Study the layout of the spreadsheet, and get a feel for how it organizes the information from the printed problem description in this text. You will see that some of the values in the spreadsheet are marked with an asterisk (*). These are usually values related to the decision variables in the problem you are solving. *You can change any value (number) that is marked with an asterisk.* When you make a change, the rest of the values (numbers) in that column are recalculated to show how a change in the value of one variable affects the others.

Making changes in values is easy. When the Spreadsheet Screen appears, you will see that one of the values in the spreadsheet is highlighted. As on the Problem Selection Screen, think of the highlighting as a pointer that shows where you are in the spreadsheet. Use the D key to move **Down**, the U key to move **Up**, the R key to move **Right**, and the L key to move **Left** until you are highlighting the value you want to change. (Note: You can also use the up, down, left and right arrow keys to move around on the screen.)

When you have highlighted the value (number) you want to change, just type in your new number. This number will show in the menu box at the bottom of the screen as you type. When you are finished typing the number, press the enter key and the other values in the spreadsheet will be recalculated to show the effect of your new value. (Note: the enter key is much like a "carriage return" key on a typewriter. It is usually larger than other keys and is located on the right side of the keyboard. Usually, a bent arrow is printed on the enter key. The diagram in Appendix A shows the normal location of the enter key.)

When you are typing numbers into the PLUS program, you type the numbers and the decimal point as you would on a typewriter. For example, a price of one thousand dollars and 50 cents would be typed as 1000.50 or just 1000.5--*using the number keys on the top row of the keyboard* and the period key for the decimal point. *Do not type in the dollar sign or the commas to indicate thousands.* Be careful not to type the letters o or l (lower case L) instead of the numbers 0 or 1.

Typing percent values is a possible point of confusion--since there are different ways to think about a percent. For example, "ten and a half" percent might be represented by 10.5 or .105. To avoid confusion, the program always expects you to enter percents using the first approach-- which is the way percents are discussed in the problems. Thus, if you want to enter the value for ten and a half percent you would type 10.5.

A set of permitted values is programmed in the computer for each problem to help prevent errors. For example, you cannot accidentally type a letter when the computer program expects a number. Or, if you type a number that is outside of the permitted range, the program will display a message in the menu box. Just read the message--to see what range of values are permitted--and then use the backspace key to erase what you have typed. (Note: The backspace key is usually toward the right side of the top row of the keyboard--along with the number keys--and usually it is marked with a left-pointing bold arrow. See Appendix A.) After you use the backspace key to erase what you typed earlier, retype a new number that is in the permitted range--and then press the enter key to recompute the spreadsheet.

For example, if you try to type -10.00 as the price of a product, the menu box might display a message that you can only enter a value that is greater than 1 and less than 20 for that variable. (It doesn't make sense to set the price as a negative number!) You could then backspace to erase what you typed, type in a new value, and finally press the enter key.

In addition to changing values (numbers) in the spreadsheet itself, the selections in the menu box have other uses. If you press the O key for "Output to printer," the current spreadsheet will be printed. (Before you press the O key, make sure that your computer has a printer, that it is plugged into both power and the computer, that it is turned on, and that the paper is loaded where you want it to start printing. The first time you use the printer, the program will ask you to type in your name. That way, each printout will have your name at the top.)

The menu box may also show the phrase "Select another Problem," with the letter P highlighted. If you press the P key, you will be returned to the Problem Selection Screen. Similarly, you may see the phrase "Do What If" with the letter W highlighted. If you press the W key, you will see a new screen that starts a What If analysis.

What If Analysis

The "What If" part of the program allows you to study in more detail the effect of changing the value of a particular variable. It systematically changes the value of a variable--and displays the effect that variable has on other variables. As before, all you have to do is follow the instructions in the menu box at the bottom of the screen. You could do the same thing "manually" at the Spreadsheet Screen--by entering a value for a variable, checking the effect on other variables, and then repeating the process over and over again. But the manual approach is time consuming and requires you to keep track of the results after each change. A What If analysis does all this very quickly and presents the results on the screen.

Now, let's go through the What If analysis part of the PLUS program step-by-step. Remember that you don't have to memorize this. The menu box will remind you what to do and you can press the H key (for help) to get additional detail while you are using the program. You start a What If analysis by pressing the W key when "Do What If" is an option in the menu box. The Select Value to Vary Screen will appear. It shows the values for those variables which you can change (ones which are marked with an asterisk on the original Spreadsheet Screen). One value on the Select Value to Vary Screen will be highlighted. As with other screens, you can use the D, U, R, or L keys (or the up, down, right, or left arrow keys) to "move" the highlighting to some other variable. When the value (number) you want to change is highlighted, simply press the space bar (the long key across the bottom center of the keyboard). The letter V will appear beside that value--to remind you what variable you have selected to vary.

The menu box at the bottom of the screen will then prompt you to type in a new minimum value for that variable. It will also show a suggested minimum value. This suggested minimum value is usually 20% smaller than the value from the initial spreadsheet. If you press the enter key at this point, this suggested value will be used as the minimum value in the analysis. You might want to do this your first time through to get some quick results. Later, you can type in your own minimum value in the same way as you do in the Spreadsheet Screen. Remember that you can use the backspace key to correct any errors. Press the enter key when you are finished typing.

Next you will be prompted to provide the largest value for the analysis. Here again, you can accept the program's suggested maximum value by pressing the enter key. Or if you wish, you can type in your own value.

After you have entered the minimum and maximum values for the variable you want to change, the screen will change to the Select Values to Display Screen. You will be prompted to select the variables for which you want summary results to be displayed. Typically, you will want to display the results (computed values) for variables that will be affected by the variable you change. Remember the example we used earlier. If you had specified that price was going to vary, you might want to display total revenue--to see how it changes at different price levels.

You select a variable to display in the same way that you select the variable you are going to change. Use the arrow keys to move from one value (number) to another. The highlighting moves to show you where you are. If you want the values of the highlighted variable to appear in the results table, press the space bar. The letter D will appear beside that value--as a reminder of the variable you selected to be displayed. If you change your mind, you can press the space bar again to "unselect" the highlighted value. The D will disappear--and that variable will not be displayed in the results table.

You can use this approach to select up to three variables to be displayed as the output of a What If analysis. When you have completed this step, you will see a V beside the variable you chose to vary, and a D beside one, two or three variables that you want to display.

Now you can let the computer take over. In the menu box at the bottom of the screen you will see the phrase "Analyze and Display Data," and the letter A will be highlighted. If you press the A key, the results of the What

If analysis will appear on the screen. Each row in the first column of the table will show a different value for the variable you wanted to change. The minimum value you specified will be in the first row. The maximum value will be in the bottom row. Evenly spaced values between the minimum and maximum will be in the middle rows. The other columns show the computed values for the variables you selected to display.

At this point you will want to study the results of your analysis. As with the Spreadsheet Screen, you can output a printed copy of the results. The menu box shows other possibilities. If you continue with the What If analysis, the Select Value to Vary Screen will reappear. The screen will show the values you selected in the previous analysis. The value you varied before will be highlighted. You can select the same value again by pressing the space bar, or highlight and select another value. If you want to display the values you selected before, press the A key (Analyze and Display Data). Or, you can "Clear" those selections by pressing the C key and then you can highlight and select new values to display.

At any point in the What If analysis, you can return to the Spreadsheet Screen. From there you can make additional changes in the values in the spreadsheet, do a new What If analysis, or select another problem to work. When you are finished, you can Quit the program by pressing the Q key.

Appendix B--which follows Appendix A's description of the computer keyboard--gives additional tips on the PLUS program. You will probably want to look through it after you have done some work with the practice problem. For now, however, you're probably tired of reading instructions. So work a problem or two. It's easier and faster to use the program than to read about it! Give it a try, and don't be afraid to experiment. If you have problems, remember that the H key will bring you Help in a hurry.

APPENDIX A--The Computer Keyboard

Exhibit A on the next page is a diagram of a typical keyboard for an IBM PC computer. Other computers will have a similar layout. A computer keyboard is very much like the keyboard on a normal typewriter. However, a computer keyboard usually has a few keys that are not on a typewriter.

The shaded area in Exhibit A shows the keys on the IBM keyboard that are like the keys on a regular typewriter. Included in this set of keys are the number keys you will use to type values into the spreadsheet program. Also included are the keys for the letters of the alphabet. You will sometimes press a letter key to tell the PLUS program that you want to execute a command that appears in the menu box at the bottom of the screen. For example, you press the H key to see a screen with additional help information. The space bar runs across the bottom of this part of the keyboard. The menu box will sometimes tell you to press this space bar.

In the upper right-hand corner of the shaded area in Exhibit A is a key with an arrow pointing to the left. This is the backspace key. If you are typing in a number and make a mistake, you can press this key to erase what you have typed. Then just retype the number you want.

Under the backspace key is the enter key. It is usually marked with a bent arrow. It is like the carriage return key on a typewriter. After you have typed in a number, you press the enter key to tell the computer to go on.

To the right of the shaded area on the keyboard is a set of keys which look like the keypad on a calculator. Some of these keys are marked with numbers. Several of the numbered keys will also be marked in other ways: with arrows, or the letters "PgUp," "PgDn." These keys can be used to send special information to the PLUS computer program. You can press an arrow key to move the highlighting on the screen in the direction of the arrow. If a small arrow appears on the screen, you can also use these keys to bring additional information onto the screen. "PgUp" and "PgDn" are abbreviations for "page up" and "page down." They can be used like the up and down arrow keys--but they move you around on the screen faster. The best way to understand what they do is to try them on a screen when you see the small arrow at the top or bottom of the screen. If the arrow is pointing down, try the PgDn key. If it points up, use the PgUp key.

There is one "trick" with this set of special keys. Note that one of them is labeled "Num Lock." It is like the key on a typewriter that locks the keyboard so that it types only capital letters. Once the Num Lock key has been pressed (even if by accident), the special keys type numbers.

Exhibit A: Diagram of a Typical Keyboard for an IBM Personal Computer

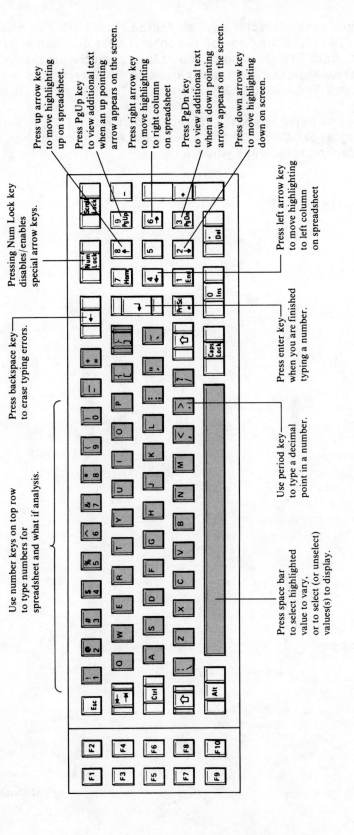

Use number keys on top row to type numbers for spreadsheet and what if analysis.

Press backspace key to erase typing errors.

Pressing Num Lock key disables/enables special arrow keys.

Press up arrow key to move highlighting up on spreadsheet.

Press PgUp key to view additional text when an up pointing arrow appears on the screen.

Press right arrow key to move highlighting to right column on spreadsheet

Press PgDn key to view additional text when a down pointing arrow appears on the screen.

Press down arrow key to move highlighting down on screen.

Press left arrow key to move highlighting to left column on spreadsheet

Press enter key when you are finished typing a number.

Use period key to type a decimal point in a number.

Press space bar to select highlighted value to vary, or to select (or unselect) value(s) to display.

To return to the "special key" mode, the Num Lock key must be pressed again. Then, pressing one of the special keys does not type a number, but instead sends information to the PLUS computer program. If you try to use the special keys and the highlighting on the screen does not move, press the Num Lock key once and try again.

The computer keyboard includes other special keys--but you don't have to worry about them. If you press these keys you will just hear a beep--a reminder to check what you are doing.

APPENDIX B--Tips on Using the PLUS Program

This appendix gives a few hints that may help you use the PLUS program.

1. The PLUS computer program is designed to work on IBM personal computers (microcomputers) and other "true" IBM-compatible microcomputers with at least 128K of memory. Almost all IBM computers have this much memory. But you don't have to know how much memory your computer has. The program will tell you if your computer doesn't have enough memory to make the program work.

2. Some values appear in the spreadsheet as whole numbers, and others appear with one or more digits to the right of a decimal point. For example, dollar values usually have two digits to the right of the decimal point--indicating how many "cents" are involved. A value indicating, say, number of customers, however, will appear as a whole number.

When you are doing arithmetic by hand (or with a calculator) you sometimes have to make decisions about how much detail is necessary. For example, if you divide 13 by 3 the answer is 4.33, 4.333, 4.3333, 4.3333 or perhaps 4.33333, depending on how important it is to be precise. Usually we round off the number to keep things manageable. Similarly, computers usually display results after rounding off the numbers. This has the potential to create confusion and seeming inaccuracy when many calculations are involved. If the computer uses a lot of detail in its calculations and then displays intermediate results after rounding off, the numbers may appear to be inconsistent. To illustrate this, let's extend the example above. If you multiply 4.33 times 2640, you get 11431.20. But if you multiply 4.333 by 2640, you get 11439.12. To make it easier for you to check relationships between the values on a spreadsheet, the PLUS program does not use a lot of "hidden detail" in calculations. If it rounds off a number to display it in the spreadsheet, the rounded number is used in subsequent calculations. It would be easy for the computer to keep track of all of the detail in its calculations--but that would make it harder for you to check the results yourself. If you check the results on a spreadsheet (with "outside" calculations) and find that your numbers are close but do not match exactly, it is probably because you are making different decisions about rounding than were programmed into PLUS.

3. The initial spreadsheet for each problem gives the "starting values" for the problem. While working a problem, you will often change one or more of the starting values to a new number. A changed value stays in effect--unless you change it again. This is a handy feature. But, after you have made several changes you may not be able to remember the starting values. There is a simple solution--you can return to the Problem Selection Screen,

highlight the problem again, and press the P key. The spreadsheet will appear with the original set of starting values. If you return to the Problem Selection Screen after working on a problem--but then change your mind and decide you want to return to the spreadsheet screen that contains the changes you had already made--just press the C key (you will see from the menu box at the bottom of the screen that this is short for "Continue with Last problem.")

Remember that a value stays changed until you change it again. Some of the questions that accompany the problems ask you to evaluate results associated with different sets of values. It's good practice to check that you have entered all the correct values on a spreadsheet before interpreting the results.

4. The Help information and the other menu box choices at the bottom should keep you from having problems. You can also use the Quit command to exit from PLUS and start over. However, if you get really stuck you always have an "emergency exit." You can turn off the computer--wait 20 seconds or so--and then turn it on again. This should not be necessary! But, it's nice to know that you can start over again without hurting the program or the computer.

5. The PLUS program was designed and tested to be easy to use and error free. In fact, it is programmed to help prevent the user from making typing errors. But, it is impossible to anticipate every possible combination of numbers which you might enter--and some combinations of numbers can cause problems. For example, a certain combination of numbers might result in an instruction for the computer to divide a number by zero--which is a mathematical impossibility! When a problem of this sort occurs, the word ERROR will appear in the spreadsheet (or in the What If results) instead of a number. If this happens, you should recheck the numbers in the spreadsheet and redo the analysis--to make certain that the numbers you typed in were what you intended. That should straighten out the problem in almost every case. Yet, with any computer program there can be hidden "bugs" that only surface in unusual situations--or on certain computers. Thus, if you think you have found a bug, we would like to know so that we can track down the source of the difficulty.

Computer-Aided Problems

1. Revenue, Cost, and Profit Relationships

This problem introduces you to spreadsheet analysis--and gets you started with the PLUS computer program. This problem is quite simple. In fact, you could easily work it without the PLUS program. But by starting with a simple problem, you will learn how to use the program more quickly and see how it will help you with more complicated problems.

A firm must make a profit to survive--so a good marketing manager thinks about profit--and what variables affect profit. A good place to start is with the relationship: Profit = Revenue - Total Cost. But, usually we want more detail. For example, we might want to be able to analyze what combination of price and quantity produces the Revenue--by substituting in the relationship: Revenue = (Selling Price) x (Quantity Sold).

Often we want to look at cost in more detail too. But, to keep this problem simple, we will just focus on Total Cost.

For this problem, the simple profit, revenue, and cost relationships discussed above are programmed into the computer. In addition, specific cost, quantity, and price data for two firms are given in the Spreadsheet Screen. Use the program to answer the questions below. Remember, you can press the H key to get help whenever you need it. Record your answers on a separate sheet of paper.

a. From the Spreadsheet Screen, what is the revenue for Firm A? For Firm B? What is the profit for Firm A? For Firm B?

b. Change Firm A's price to 9.25. Note which other values in the spreadsheet change. At the $9.25 price, what is Firm A's revenue? Its total cost? Its profit (or loss)? Using values from the spreadsheet, show (on your paper) the calculations that prove that the program has given you the correct values.

c. Prepare a table for Firm B--on your separate sheet of paper--with column headings for three variables: quantity sold, revenue, and profit. For Firm B, show the value for revenue and profit for different values of quantity sold-- starting at a minimum of 800 units sold and adding 40 units to the quantity until you reach a maximum of 1,200 units sold. At what quantity does Firm B make only $80.00? (Hint: Use the What If analysis to compute the new values. Start by selecting "units sold" for Firm B as the value to change. Select Firm B's revenue and profit as the values to display.)

2. Target Marketing

Marko, Inc.'s managers are comparing the profitability of a target marketing strategy with a mass marketing "strategy." The spreadsheet gives information about both approaches.

The mass marketing strategy is aiming at a much bigger market. But a smaller percent of the consumers in the market will actually buy this product--because not everyone needs or can afford it. Moreover, because this marketing mix is not tailored to specific needs, Marko will get a smaller share of the business from those who do buy than it would with a more targeted marketing mix.

Just trying to reach the mass market will take more promotion and require more middlemen in more locations--so promotion costs and distribution costs are higher than with the target marketing strategy. On the other hand, the cost of producing each unit is higher with the target marketing strategy--to build in a more satisfying set of features. But, because the more targeted marketing mix is trying to satisfy the needs of a specific target market, those customers will be willing to pay a higher price.

In the spreadsheet, "quantity sold" (by the firm) is equal to the number of people in the market who will actually buy one each of the product-- multiplied by the share of those purchases won by the firm's marketing mix. Thus, a change in the size of the market, the percent of people who purchase, or the share captured by the firm will affect quantity sold. And a change in quantity sold will affect total revenue, total cost, and profit.

a. On a piece of paper, show the calculations that prove that the spreadsheet "total profit" value for the target marketing strategy is correct. (Hint: remember to multiply unit production cost and unit distribution cost by the quantity sold.) Which approach seems better--target marketing or mass marketing? Why?

b. If the target marketer could find a way to reduce distribution cost per unit by $.25, how much would profit increase?

c. If Marko, Inc. decided to use the target marketing strategy and better marketing mix decisions increased its share of purchases from 50 percent to 60 percent--without increasing costs--what would happen to total profit? What does this analysis suggest about the importance of a marketing manager knowing enough about his target markets to be an effective target marketer?

3. Segmenting Customers

The marketing manager for Micro Software Company is seeking new market opportunities. He has used a market segmentation approach to narrow the "word processing" market down to three segments: "the fearful typists," "the power-users," and "the professional specialists." The fearful typists don't know much about computers--they just want a fast way to type letters and simple reports without errors. They don't need a lot of special features. They want simple instructions and a program that's easy to learn. The power users know a lot about computers, use them often, and want a word processing program with many special features. All computer programs seem easy to them--so they aren't worried about learning to use the various features. The professional specialists have jobs that require a lot of writing. They don't know much about computers but are willing to learn. They want special features needed for their work--but only if they aren't too hard to learn and use. The marketing manager prepared the following table summarizing the importance of each of three key needs in the three segments:

	Importance of Need (1=not important; 10=very important)		
Segment	Features	Easy to Use	Easy to Learn
Fearful Typists	3	8	9
Power Users	9	2	2
Professional Specialists	7	5	6

A sample of potential customers were asked to rate the importance (to each of them) of each of these three needs. The manager prepared a spreadsheet to help him cluster (aggregate) each person into one of the segments--along with other similar people. Each person's ratings are entered in the spreadsheet and the clustering procedure computes a similarity score that shows how similar (a low score) or dissimilar (a high score) the person is to the typical person in each of the segments. The manager can then "aggregate" potential customers into the segment that is most similar (that is, the one with the lowest similarity score).

a. The ratings for a potential customer appear on the first spreadsheet. Into which segment would you aggregate this person?

b. The responses for 7 potential customers are listed on the next page. Enter the ratings for a customer in the spreadsheet and then write down the similarity score for each segment. Repeat the process of each customer. Based on your analysis, indicate the segment into which you would aggregate each customer. Indicate the size (number of customers) of each segment.

Potential		Importance of Need*		
Customer	Features	Easy to Use	Easy to Learn	Type of Computer
A.	8	1	2	IBM
B.	6	6	5	Amiga
C.	4	9	8	McIntosh
D.	2	6	7	McIntosh
E.	5	6	5	Amiga
F.	8	3	1	IBM
G.	4	6	8	McIntosh

*Note: 1=not important; 10=very important

c. *In the interview, each potential customer was also asked what type of computer he would be using. The responses are shown in the table along with the ratings. Group the responses based on the customer's segment. If you were targeting the fearful typist segment, what type of computer would you focus on when developing your software?*

d. *Based on your analysis, which customer would you say is* least *like any of the segments. Briefly explain the reason for your choice.*

4. Company Resources

Mediquip, Inc. produces medical equipment--and uses its own sales force to sell the equipment to hospitals. Recently, several hospitals have asked Mediquip to develop a laser-beam "scalpel" for eye surgery. Mediquip has the needed resources--and it is likely that 200 hospitals will buy the equipment. But Mediquip managers have heard that Laser Technologies-- another quality producer--is thinking of competing for the same business. Mediquip has other good opportunities it could pursue--so it wants to see if it would have a competitive advantage over Laser Tech.

Mediquip and Laser Tech are similar in many ways--but there are also differences. Laser Technologies already produces key parts that are needed for the new laser product--so its production costs would be lower. It would cost Mediquip more to design the product--and getting parts from outside suppliers would result in higher production costs.

On the other hand, Mediquip has marketing strengths. It already has a good reputation with hospitals--and its sales force calls only on hospitals. Mediquip thinks that each of its current sales reps could spend some time selling the new product--and that sales territories could be adjusted so that only five more sales reps would be needed for good coverage in the market.

In contrast, Laser Tech's sales reps now only call on industrial customers. So it would have to add 14 reps to cover the hospitals.

Most hospitals have budget pressures--so the supplier with the lowest price is likely to get a larger share of the business. But Mediquip knows that either supplier's price will be set high enough to cover the added costs of designing, producing and selling the new product--and leave something for profit.

After getting information on its own likely costs and estimates of Laser Tech's costs, Mediquip has set up a spreadsheet to evaluate the proposed new product.

a. The initial spreadsheet results are based on Mediquip's assumption that it could get at least 50 percent of the market. At that level, does Mediquip have a competitive advantage over Laser Tech? Explain.

b. Because of economies of scale, both suppliers' average cost per machine will vary--depending on the quantity sold. If Mediquip only had 45 percent of the market and Laser Tech had 55 percent, how would their costs compare? What if Mediquip had 55 percent of the market and Laser Tech had only 45 percent? What conclusion do you draw from these analyses?

c. It is possible that Laser Tech may not enter the market. If Mediquip has 100 percent of the market and can get a better source of supply so that its cost of producing one unit is reduced to $6,500, what price would cover all its costs and contribute $1,125 to profit for every machine sold? What does this suggest about the desirability of finding your own unsatisfied target markets? Explain.

5. Marketing Research

Texmac, Inc. has an idea for a new type of weaving machine that could replace the machines now used by many textile manufacturers. Texmac has done a telephone survey to estimate how many are now in use. Respondents using the present machines were also asked if they would buy the improved machine at a price of $10,000.

Texmac researchers identified a population of about 5,000 textile manufacturers who might be customers. A sample of these were surveyed, and 500 firms responded. Thus the total potential market is about 10 times larger than the respondents.

Texmac thinks the sample responders are representative of the total population, but the marketing manager realizes that estimates based on a sample may not be exact when applied to the whole population. He wants to see how sampling "error" would affect profit estimates. Data for his problem appear in the spreadsheet. Quantity estimates for the whole market are computed from the sample estimates. These quantity estimates are used in computing likely sales, costs, and profit contribution.

a. If there are really 5,200 potential textile manufacturer customers--not 5,000-- how does that affect the total quantity estimate and expected revenue and profit contribution?

b. If the actual number of old machines in the market is really 200 per 500 firms--not 220 as estimated from survey responses--how much would this affect the expected profit contribution?

c. Forty percent of the sample respondents said they would replace their old machines. But the marketing manager knows he can't be sure that they will buy the replacement machine until it is available. He estimates the proportion that will replace the old machine may vary between 36 percent and 44 percent. Use the What If analysis to prepare a table that shows how expected quantity and profit contribution changes when the sample percent varies between a minimum of 36 and a maximum of 44 percent. What does this analysis suggest about the use of estimates from marketing research samples? (Note: Use 220 as the estimate of the number of old machines.)

6. Demographic Analysis

Stylco, Inc. produces clothing for children and adults. Most buyers of the adult styles are 45-64 years old. Children's styles are aimed at ages 5 to 17. As the number of children in this age group has dropped, sales of children's clothing have dropped too. But sales of adult styles have increased.

To get a long-run view of these trends, Stylco's marketing manager looked at 1981 Statistics Canada Census data by age group. He also got estimates of 1991 population and the expected growth rate for each group through the year 2001. He has entered the estimates in a spreadsheet to estimate population distribution for the year 2001.

Based on an analysis of past sales data, he learned that the number of items the firm sells is in direct proportion to the size of each age group. For many years, this ratio of units sold to population has been .001. He also entered this ratio in the spreadsheet--to see how changes in population is likely to affect units sold. Finally, he has determined the average profit earned for each item sold, and entered that--to get an idea about possible

McCarthy, Shapiro & Perreault

future profits from each line. All of the data, and the relationships discussed above, are programmed into the spreadsheet.

a. Briefly compare the estimated profit data for 1991 and 2001 as it appears on the initial spreadsheet. What are the implications of these and other data in the spreadsheet for Stylco's marketing strategy planning?

b. Some experts think that percent growth in the children's group for the 1991-2001 period will be higher than the Statistics Canada estimate the marketing manager used for the spreadsheet. If the percent growth is actually 13.0 percent, not 10.2 percent as assumed, what is the affect on profits from the children's line?

c. The marketing manager thinks that competition may increase in lines targeted to the 45-64 age group. He thinks his "ratio of units sold to population" may decrease as more firms compete for this business. Use the What If analysis to prepare a table showing how profits and "percent of profit" from this group might change as the "ratio of units sold to population" varies between a minimum of 0.0003 and a maximum of .0013. Explain the implications to the firm.

7. Selective Processes

Submag, Inc. uses direct mail promotion to sell magazine subscriptions at a bargain price. Each mailing piece costs between $.30 and $.40. This includes the cost of the computerized mailing list, supplies, mailing, and other expenses. Each order averages $3.12--but not every consumer who is sent a mailer buys a subscription. Some mailers are returned by the post office because the person has moved. In addition, selective exposure is a problem. Some people who receive the mailer never see the offer because they toss out "junk mail" without even opening the envelope.

Selective perception influences some of those who do open the mailer. Many see the subscription service as too risky and have no further interest. Many of those who see the message as intended are interested but forget to send in the subscription order (selective retention).

Submag's marketing manager is deciding between one of two computerized mailing lists. The lists come from different sources and include addresses for different types of consumers. Researchers from the mailing list firms have provided some estimates of the responses that can be expected from the two lists. Submag's marketing manager has set up a spreadsheet to help decide which list to buy.

a. If you were Submag's marketing manager, which of the two lists would you use to reach your target market? Why?

b. Given the amount of "wasted" promotion because of consumers' selective processes, approximately how many mailers will Submag have to mail--using the best list--to earn a profit of at least $3,500?

c. For an added $.01 per mailing, Submag can add a reply card that will reduce the percent of consumers who forget to send in the subscription order to 45 percent. Would it be worth the higher cost to include the reply card? Explain.

8. Vendor Analysis

CompuTech, Inc. produces accessories for microcomputers. It is evaluating two possible suppliers of electronic memory chips.

The chips do basically the same job, but it's difficult to control the quality of the chips and some are always defective. Both suppliers will replace defective chips. But the only practical way to test for a defective chip is to assemble the whole product and see if it works. When a chip is defective at that point, it costs $2.00 in labor time to replace it. One supplier guarantees that 99 percent of its chips will work. The other guarantees only 98 percent, but its price is lower.

The supplier with the lower defective rate has been able to improve its quality because it uses a heavier plastic case to hold the chip. This is not a big problem for CompuTech, but the heavier case requires a more expensive connector.

Other differences between suppliers relate to location. The lower cost supplier is overseas--and delays in filling orders are sometimes a problem. To ensure that a sufficient supply is on hand to keep production going, CompuTech will have to maintain a larger inventory--and this will increase its inventory costs. In addition, CompuTech will pay for transporting the chips from the supplier--and the cost is higher for overseas shipments.

To make its vendor analysis easier, CompuTech's purchasing agent has entered data about the two suppliers on a spreadsheet. He based his estimates on the quantity he thinks he will need over a full year. Inventory costs are figured as a percentage of the total order cost.

a. Based on the results shown in the initial spreadsheet, which supplier do you think CompuTech should select? Why?

b. CompuTech estimates it will need 100,000 chips--if sales go as expected. But if sales are slow, fewer chips will be needed. Supplier 1's price per chip will be $1.95 each if CompuTech buys less than 90,000 during the year. If CompuTech only needs 84,500 chips, which supplier would be more economical?

c. If the actual purchase quantity will be 84,500 and Supplier 1's price is $1.95, what is the highest price at which Supplier 2 will still be the lower cost vendor for CompuTech? [Hint: You can enter price values in the spreadsheet--or use the What If analysis to vary Supplier 2's price and display the total costs for both vendors.]

9. Branding Decision

Farm Fresh Dairy, Inc. produces and sells Farm Fresh brand condensed milk to grocery retailers. The regular price to retailers is $8.88 a case (24 cans). FoodWorld--a fast growing supermarket chain and Farm Fresh's largest customer--buys 20,000 cases of Farm Fresh's condensed milk a year.

FoodWorld is proposing that Farm Fresh produce condensed milk to be sold with the FoodWorld brand name. FoodWorld wants to buy the same total quantity as it does now, but it wants half with the Farm Fresh brand and half with the FoodWorld brand. FoodWorld wants its brand in a different can that will stack on shelves easier. (In fact, FoodWorld has a supplier who will provide the new can at $.01 less than Farm Fresh pays for a can now.) And FoodWorld will provide pre-printed labels with its brand name--which will save Farm Fresh $.02 a can.

Farm Fresh does its own promotion to increase familiarity with the Farm Fresh brand. In addition, retailers also advertise the brand in their local areas. Farm Fresh helps pay for this local advertising by giving retailers an advertising allowance of $.25 a case. FoodWorld has agreed to give up the advertising allowance for its own brand, but it is only willing to pay $7.40 a case for the milk that will be sold with the FoodWorld brand name. It will continue under the "old terms" for the rest of its purchases.

Farm Fresh's marketing manager is considering the FoodWorld proposal. He has entered cost and revenue data on a spreadsheet--so he can see more clearly how the proposal might affect revenues and profits.

a. Based on the data in the initial spreadsheet, how will Farm Fresh profits be affected if it accepts the FoodWorld proposal?

b. Farm Fresh's marketing manager worries that FoodWorld will find another producer for the FoodWorld brand if Farm Fresh rejects the proposal. This would immediately reduce sales by 10,000 cases. FoodWorld might even stop buying from Farm Fresh altogether. What would happen to profits in these two situations?

c. FoodWorld is growing rapidly and Farm Fresh's marketing manager expects that its purchases will increase to 25,000 cases by the end of next year. But he also thinks that then FoodWorld may stop buying the Farm Fresh brand and want all 25,000 cases to carry the FoodWorld brand. How will this affect profits? (Hint: Enter the new quantities in the "proposal" column of the spreadsheet.)

d. What should Farm Fresh do? Why?

10. Growth Stage Competition

AgriChem, Inc. has introduced an innovative new product--a combination fertilizer, weed killer, and insecticide that makes it much easier for soybean farmers to produce a profitable crop. The product introduction was successful--and AgriChem's profits are increasing. Total market demand is expected to grow at a rate of 200,000 units a year for the next five years. Even so, AgriChem's marketing manager is concerned about what will happen to his sales and profits during this period.

Based on past experience with similar situations, the marketing manager expects a new competitor to enter the market during each of the next five years. He thinks this competitive pressure will drive prices down about 6 percent a year. Further, although the total market is growing, he knows that new competitors will chip away at his market share--even with the 10 percent a year increase he has planned for his promotion budget. In spite of the competitive pressure, the marketing manager is sure that familiarity with AgriChem's brand will help it hold a large share of the total market-- and give AgriChem greater economies of scale than competitors. In fact, he expects that the ratio of profit to dollar sales for AgriChem should be about 10 percent higher than for competitors.

AgriChem's marketing manager has decided the best way to "get a handle" on the situation is to organize the data in a spreadsheet. He has set up the spreadsheet so he can change the "years in the future" value and see what is likely to happen to AgriChem and the rest of the industry. The starting spreadsheet shows the current situation.

a. *Compare AgriChem's market share and profit for this year with what is expected next year--given the marketing manager's current assumptions. What is he expecting?*

b. *Prepare a table showing AgriChem's expected profit, and expected industry revenue and profit, for the current year and the next five years. Briefly explain what happens to industry sales and profits and why. (Hint: Change the "number of years in the future" value in the spreadsheet, and study the various factors that affect revenue and profits.)*

c. *If market demand grows faster than expected--say, at 280,000 units a year-- what will happen to AgriChem's profits, and industry revenues and profits over the next five years?*

11. Intensive vs. Selective Distribution

Hydropump, Inc. produces and sells high quality pumps to industrial customers. Its marketing research shows a growing market for a similar type of pump aimed at final consumers--for use with home hot-tubs and jacuzzi tubs. Hydropump will have to develop new channels of distribution to reach this target market because most consumers rely on a retailer for advice about the combination of tub, pump, heater, and related plumbing fixtures they need. Hydropump's marketing manager is trying to decide between intensive and selective distribution. With intensive distribution, he would try to sell through all the plumbing supply, swimming pool, and hot-tub retailers who will carry the pump. He estimates that about 5,600 suitable retailers would be willing to carry a new pump. With selective distribution, he would focus on about 280 of the best hot-tub dealers (two or three in the hundred largest metropolitan areas.).

Intensive distribution would require Hydropump to do more mass selling--primarily advertising in home renovation magazines--to help stimulate consumer familiarity with the brand and convince retailers that Hydropump equipment will sell. The price to the retailer might have to be lower too (to permit a bigger markup) so they will be motivated to sell Hydropump rather than some other brand offering a smaller markup.

With intensive distribution, each Hydropump sales rep could probably handle about 300 retailers effectively. With selective distribution, each sales rep could handle only about 70 retailers, because more merchandising help would be necessary. Managing the smaller sales force and fewer retailers--with the selective approach-- would require less manager overhead cost.

Going to all suitable and available retailers would make the pump available through about 20 times as many retailers and have the potential of reaching more customers. However, many customers shop at more than one retailer before making a final choice--so selective distribution would reach almost as many potential customers. Further, if Hydropump is using selective distribution, it would get more attention for its pump--and a larger share of pump purchases--at each retailer.

Hydropump's marketing manager has decided to use a spreadsheet to analyze the benefits and costs of intensive versus selective distribution.

a. Based on the initial spreadsheet, which approach seems to be the most sensible for Hydropump? Why?

b. If Hydropump has to spend $100,000 on mass selling to be able to recruit the retailers it wants for selective distribution, would selective or intensive distribution be more profitable?

c. With intensive distribution, how large a share (percent) of the retailer's total unit sales would Hydropump have to capture to sell enough pumps to earn $200,000 profit?

12. Mass-merchandising

The manager of PlayTime Toy Store is sure a new type of toy will be a big seller in his area. But two brands of the toy are available. So he must decide which to sell, since he doesn't have enough shelf space to stock both. In fact, he wants to use as little shelf space as possible for the toy--to save space for other good sellers.

PlayTime's manager asked his wholesaler how many of these toys he may sell in some time period. The wholesaler reported that different stores were adding different dollar markups to the cost and lower markups usually sold larger quantities. Detailed information was supplied for the retailer to analyze.

The wholesaler also advised PlayTime that at least 5 of the toys should show on a shelf--to get enough attention to spark sales. Either toy's package will use the full depth of a standard shelf, but the "face" of one package is wider than the other.

PlayTime's manager must decide which brand to carry and what markup to use. Relevant information, including the wholesaler's quantity estimates based on different markups, is in the spreadsheet. (Note: "Contribution" to profit is equal to the markup per toy times the number of toys sold at that markup.)

a. Based on the different markup and "quantity sold" combinations provided by the wholesaler, what markup on Brand A would result in the largest contribution to profit? What markup on Brand B would result in the largest contribution? Based on profit contribution, which brand would you recommend? (Hint: Change the starting markup and quantity values to the combinations received from the wholesaler.)

b. Given the "best" margin and quantity estimates from (a) above, which brand will earn the highest "contribution" per inch of shelf "facing" (assuming five package displays as suggested by the wholesaler)?

c. Which brand and markup would you recommend? Why?

13. Merchant vs. Agent Wholesaler

Art Glass Productions, a producer of decorative glass gift items, wants to expand into a new territory and is trying to decide whether to work with a merchant wholesaler who specializes in gift items or a manufacturers' agent who calls on many of the gift shops in this territory.

Art Glass makes a variety of glass items, but the cost of making an item is usually about the same--$5.20 a unit. The items would sell to the merchant wholesaler at $12.00 each--and his price to retailers would be $14.00--leaving him with a $2.00 markup to cover his costs and profit. There is only one good merchant wholesaler in the territory, and he has agreed to carry the line only if Art Glass is willing to advertise in a trade magazine aimed at gift store owners. These ads will cost $8,000 a year.

The manufacturers' agent would cover all of his own expenses, and would earn 8 percent of the $14.00 price per unit charged the gift shops. Individual orders would be shipped to the retail gift shops by Art Glass-- using United Parcel Service. Art Glass would absorb the UPS charges-- which would be about $2.00 per item. In contrast, the merchant wholesaler would anticipate demand and place larger orders in advance. This would reduce Art Glass' shipping costs to about $.60 a unit.

Art Glass' marketing manager thinks that the manufacturers' agent would only be able to sell about 75 percent as many items as the merchant wholesaler--since he doesn't have time to call on all of the smaller shops. On the other hand, the merchant wholesaler's demand for $8,000 worth of supporting advertising requires a significant outlay.

The marketing manager has decided to use a spreadsheet to determine how large sales would have to be to make it more profitable to use the merchant wholesaler. The manager also wants to see how the different arrangements would contribute to his profits at different sales levels.

a. *Given the expected sales quantities on the initial spreadsheet, which type of wholesaler would contribute the most profit to Art Glass Productions?*

b. *If demand were lower than expected, so that the merchant wholesaler was only able to sell 3,000 units (or the agent only 2,250 units), which wholesaler would contribute the most to Art Glass' profits? (Note: Assume that the merchant wholesaler only buys what it can sell, i.e., it doesn't carry extra inventory beyond what is needed to meet demand.)*

c. *Prepare a table showing how the two wholesalers' contribution to profit compare as the quantity demanded (sold) varies from 3,500 units to 4,500 units for the merchant wholesaler and 75 percent of these numbers for the manufacturers' agent. Discuss these results. (Note: Use the What If analysis to vary the quantity demanded (sold) by the merchant wholesaler, and the program will compute 75 percent of that quantity as the estimate of what the agent will sell.)*

14. Total Distribution Cost

Bay Shore Company is considering two possible physical distribution systems. If it uses airfreight, transportation costs are $3.00 a unit, and its cost of carrying inventory is 5 percent of total annual sales dollars. Or it can ship by railroad for $1.00 a unit. But rail transport will require renting space at four regional warehouses--at $10,000 a year each. Inventory carrying cost with this system will be 10 percent of total annual sales dollars. The product will sell for $20.00 regardless of which PD system is used.

a. *If Bay Shore expects to sell 20,000 units a year, what are the total PD costs for each of the systems?*

b. *What would happen to total PD costs if inventory carrying cost changed to 7 percent for airfreight, and to 8 percent for railroads? Which alternative would you suggest then? Why?*

c. *If the system using airfreight required space in a warehouse that cost $5,000 a year, which alternative would you select? Why?*

15. Sales Promotion

As a community service, disk jockeys from radio station WXYZ have formed a basketball team to help raise money for local non-profit organizations. The "host" organization finds or fields a competing team, and charges $5.00 admission to the game. Money from ticket sales goes to the non-profit organization.

Ticket sales have been disappointing at recent games--averaging only about 300 people per game. When WXYZ's marketing manager heard about the problem, he suggested using sales promotion to improve ticket sales. The PTA for the local high school--the sponsor for the next game--likes his idea but is concerned that its budget doesn't include any promotion money. The marketing manager has tried to help them by reviewing his idea in more detail.

Specifically, he suggests that the PTA give a free t-shirt (printed with the school name and date of the game) to the first 500 ticket buyers. WXYZ's marketing manager thinks the t-shirt give-away will create a lot of interest--and probably double the number of tickets sold. He speculates that the PTA might even have a sell out of all 900 seats in the school gym. Further, he notes that the t-shirts will more than pay for themselves if ticket sales double.

A local firm that specializes in promotion items will supply the shirts and do the printing for $2.40 a shirt--if the PTA places an order for at least 400 shirts. The PTA thinks the idea is interesting, but wants to look at it more closely--to see what will happen if the promotion doesn't increase ticket sales. The PTA president has also suggested that they offer a choice-- $5.00 for a regular ticket or $6.00 with the special t-shirt. To help the PTA evaluate the alternatives, WXYZ's marketing manager has set up a spreadsheet with the relevant information.

a. Based on the data from the initial spreadsheet, does the t-shirt promotion look like a good idea? Why?

b. The PTA treasurer wants to know where they would stand if they ordered the t-shirts and still sold only 300 tickets. He thinks it might be safer to order the minimum number of t-shirts (400). Evaluate his suggestion.

c. Another PTA member thinks the t-shirt promotion will increase sales, but wonders if it wouldn't be better just to lower the price. He suggests $2.60 a ticket, since that is the regular price minus the cost of a t-shirt. How many tickets would the PTA have to sell at the lower price to match the money it would make if it used the t-shirt promotion and actually sold 600 tickets? (Hint:

Change the selling price in the spreadsheet, and then vary the quantity using the What If analysis.)

16. Sales Compensation

Yale, Inc.'s sales manager is trying to decide whether to pay a sales rep for a new territory with straight commission or a combination plan. He wants to evaluate possible plans--to compare the compensation costs and profitability of each. (Note: Sales reps in similar jobs at other firms make about $30,000 a year.)

The sales rep will sell two products. The sales manager is planning a higher commission for product B--because he wants it to get extra effort. He has some rough estimates of expected sales volume under the different plans--and various ideas about commission rates. The details are found in the spreadsheet. The program computes compensation--and how much the sales rep will contribute to profit. "Profit contribution" is equal to the total revenue generated by the sales rep minus sales compensation costs and the costs of producing the units.

a. How do compensation and "profit contribution" for the two plans compare if sales are 10% lower than expected? 10% higher than expected?

b. The sales manager is considering raising the commission rate on product A-- under the combination plan--to 6%. He thinks the higher commission will motivate the rep to increase sales by 10 percent. Assuming he is correct about the increase in sales, would you advise him to move ahead with the commission rate increase?

c. Prepare a table that shows what happens to sales compensation and profit contribution as quantity sold increases between 2,880 and 4,320 under the combination plan. Study your results and discuss the profit implications of increases in sales quantity under the combination plan.

17. Advertising Media

Peter Troy, owner of three Sound Haus stereo equipment stores, is deciding what advertising medium to use to promote his newest store. He has found direct mail ads effective for reaching his current customers, but he wants to attract new customers too. The best prospects are professionals in the 25-44 age range--with incomes over $38,000 a year. But only some of the people in this group are "audiophiles" who want the top-of-the-line brands he carries.

Troy has narrowed his choice to two media: an FM radio station and a biweekly magazine that focuses on entertainment in his city. Many of the readers of the magazine are out-of-town visitors interested in concerts, plays, and restaurants during their stay. They usually buy stereo equipment at home. But the magazine's audience research shows that many local professionals do subscribe to the magazine. Troy feels that ads in six issues will generate good local awareness with his target market. In addition, the magazine's color format will let him present the prestige image he wants to convey in an ad. He thinks that will help convert "aware prospects" to buyers. A local advertising agency will prepare a high impact ad for $2,000 and then Troy will pay for the magazine space.

The FM radio station targets an audience similar to Troy's own target market. He knows that repeated ads will be needed to be sure that most of his target audience is exposed to his ads. Troy thinks it will take daily ads for several months to create adequate awareness among his target market. The FM station will provide an announcer and prepare a tape of Troy's ad for a one-time fee of $200. All he has to do is tell them what the ad should say.

Both the radio station and the magazine have given Troy reports summarizing recent audience research. He has decided that putting everything together in a spreadsheet will help him make a better decision.

a. *Based on the data displayed on the initial spreadsheet, which medium would you recommend to Troy? Why?*

b. *The agency that offered to prepare Troy's magazine ad will prepare a musical radio ad for $2,500. The agency claims its ad will have much more impact than the ad the radio station will create. The ad agency claims that its ad should produce the same results as the station ad with 20 percent fewer insertions. If the agency claim is correct, would it be wise for Troy to pay the agency to produce the ad?*

c. *The agency will not guarantee that its ad will reach Troy's objective--making 80 percent of the prospects aware of the new store. He wants to see how lower levels of awareness--between 50 percent and 70 percent--would affect the advertising cost per buyer and the cost per aware prospect. Use the What If analysis to vary the percent of prospects who become aware. Prepare a table showing the effect on the two kinds of costs.*

18. Cash Discounts

Joe Tulkin owns Tulkin Wholesale Co. He sells paper, tape, file folders and other office supplies to about 120 retailers in nearby cities. His average retailer customer buys about $900 a month from him. When Tulkin started business in 1980, competing wholesalers gave retailers invoice terms of "3/10, net 30." Tulkin never gave the terms much thought--he just used the same invoice terms when he billed customers. Recently, however, Tulkin learned that some wholesalers are changing their invoice terms. In addition, he has noticed a change in the way his customers are paying their bills. In 1980, half of his customers took the 3 percent cash discount and paid their bill within 10 days. The rest were glad to have Tulkin extend credit--and waited the full 30 days to pay. Now, 90 percent of the retailers are taking the cash discount. With so many retailers taking the cash discount, it seems to have become a price reduction.

Tulkin has decided he should rethink his invoice terms. He knows he could change the percent rate on the cash discount, the number of days the discount is offered, or the number of days before the face amount is due. Changing any of these--or any combination--will change the interest rate at which a buyer is--in effect--borrowing money if he does not take the discount. Tulkin has decided that it will be easier to evaluate the effect of different invoice terms if he sets up a spreadsheet to let him change the terms and quickly see the "effective" interest rate for each change.

a. With 90 percent of Tulkin's customers now taking the discount, what is the total monthly cash discount amount?

b. If Tulkin changes his invoice terms to 1/5, net 20, what interest rate is each buyer--in effect--paying by not taking the cash discount? With these terms, would fewer buyers be likely to take the discount? Why?

c. Tulkin thinks 10 customers will switch to other wholesalers if he changes his invoice terms to 2/10, net 30, while 60 percent of the remaining customers will take the discount. What interest rate does a buyer--in effect--pay by not taking this cash discount? For this situation, what will the total gross sales (total invoice) amount be? The total cash discount? The total net sales receipts after the total cash discount? Compare Tulkin's current situation with what will happen if he changes his invoice terms to 2/10, net 30.

McCarthy, Shapiro & Perreault

19. Break-even/Profit Analysis

This problem lets you see the dynamics of break-even analysis. The starting values (costs, revenues, etc.) for this problem are from the break-even analysis example in Chapter 19, "Price Setting in the Real World," of the 5th Canadian edition of *Basic Marketing*. See Exhibit 19-8.

The first column computes a break-even point. You can change costs and prices to figure new break-even points (in units and dollars). The second column goes further. There you can specify target profit level, and the unit and dollar sales needed to achieve your target profit level will be computed. You can also estimate possible sales quantities and the program will compute costs, sales, and profits. Use this spreadsheet to answer the following questions.

a. Vary the selling price between $1.00 and $1.40. Prepare a table showing how the break-even point (in units and dollars) changes at the different price levels.

b. If you hope to earn a target profit of $15,000, how many units would you have to sell? What would total cost be? Total sales dollars? (Note: Use the right-hand ("profit analysis") column in the spreadsheet.)

c. Using the "profit analysis" column (column 2), allow your estimate of the sale quantity to vary between 64,000 and 96,000. Prepare a table that shows, for each quantity level, what happens to total cost, average cost per unit, and profit. Explain why average cost changes as it does over the different quantity values.

20. Comparing Marketing Mixes

The marketing manager for Sunco, Inc.--a producer of small appliances-- is doing some rough comparisons of the likely costs and profitability of possible marketing mixes. Data for marketing mix "B" and marketing mix "C" are in the spreadsheet.

a. If mix B resulted in sales of 8,250 units instead of 7,000, which mix would be most profitable?

b. How do the break-even quantities compare for the two mixes? (Note: Assume that selling cost and advertising cost do not vary with sales.)

c. For each mix, vary the quantity to be sold between 5,600 and 8,400. For each mix, prepare a table that shows how profit changes at the different quantity levels. Then, explain which marketing mix you would select and why.

21. Marketing Cost Analysis

This problem emphasizes the differences between the full-cost approach and contribution-margin approach to marketing cost analysis.

Tapco, Inc. currently sells two products. Sales commissions and unit costs vary with the quantity of each product sold. With the full-cost approach, Tapco's administrative and advertising costs are allocated to each product based on its share of total sales dollars. Details of Tapco's costs and other data are given in the spreadsheet. The first column shows a cost analysis based on the full-cost approach. The second column shows an analysis based on the contribution-margin approach.

a. If the number of Product A units sold were to increase by 1,000 units, what would happen to the allocated administrative expense for Product A? How would the change in sales of Product A affect the allocated administrative expense for Product B? Briefly discuss why the changes you have observed might cause conflict between the product managers of the two different products.

b. What would happen to total profits if Tapco stopped selling Product A? What happens to total profits if the firm stops selling Product B? (Hint: This would mean that the quantity sold for a particular product would be zero.)

c. If the firm dropped Product B, and increased the price of Product A by $2.00, approximately what quantity of Product A would it have to sell to earn a total profit as large as it was originally earning with both products? (Hint: Change values in the spreadsheet to reflect the changes the firm is considering, and then use the What If analysis to vary the quantity of Product A sold and display what happens to total profit.)

22. Export Opportunities

Weavco, Inc. produces and sells weaving machines to textile manufacturing firms across Canada. In the past, Weavco machines have sold well, but in recent years sales and profits have been declining. Foreign textile producers have been winning a larger share of the Canadian market. As a result, domestic producers have not been buying new equipment.

Weavco's marketing manager thinks there may be an opportunity to export weaving machines to textile firms in two major textile producing countries. Weavco would have to add a new manager to handle export responsibilities. Some marketing research would also be needed to identify target customers in two possible target countries. Weavco would also have to work with an export agent--who would handle government paperwork and arrange for international shipping. Depending on the country involved, there might also be a tariff on imported machines. And Weavco would have to work with import agents who would handle contacts with target customers. The agents receive a percentage of the final selling price. Potential demand, price competition, agent commissions and other costs vary from country to country. So the Weavco's marketing manager has set up a spreadsheet to help him evaluate the opportunity in two countries.

a. If competition in the two countries is about the same, which do you think offers the best export opportunity? Draw on data from the initial spreadsheet to explain your choice.

b. If it turned out that the import agent in Country B would only take on Weavco machines if he received a 15 percent commission, how many machines would he have to sell for Weavco to "break even" (that is, recover the money it has spent on salary for an export manager and marketing research)? How many units would he have to sell for Weavco to earn its target profit of $50,000?

c. The Canadian government is negotiating with Country A to reduce trade restrictions--and industry experts think that Country A's import tariff on the weaving equipment will be reduced. Use the What If analysis to prepare a table showing how the number of units needed to reach the target profit will be affected by different tariff amounts between $1,000 and $2,100/unit. Briefly discuss the implications of your results.